CHRISTIAN CONCEPTS FOR GROWTH AND DEVELOPMENT

PRAYER & BIBLE BAND TOPICS

SUMMER QUARTER 2025
JUNE • JULY • AUGUST

LARGE PRINT

Church Of God In Christ, INC.
PRAYER & BIBLE BAND TOPICS
SUMMER QUARTER 2025 | JUNE • JULY • AUGUST

Bishop J. Drew Sheard
Presiding Bishop

Bishop Uleses C. Henderson, Jr.
Chairman, Publishing Board

Copyright © 2024 by Church Of God In Christ, Inc. Publishing House

Unless otherwise indicated, all Scripture references are taken from the authorized King James Version of the Bible.

Scripture quotations marked AMP are taken from the Amplified® Bible, Copyright © 1954, 1958, 1962, 1964, 1965, 1987 by The Lockman Foundation. Used by permission. All rights reserved.

Scripture quotations marked ESV® are taken from The Holy Bible, English Standard Version®, Copyright © 2001 by Crossway, a publishing ministry of Good News Publishers. Used by permission. All rights reserved.

Scripture quotations marked NASB are taken from the New American Standard Bible®, Copyright © 1960, 1962, 1963, 1968, 1971, 1972, 1973, 1975, 1977, 1995 by The Lockman Foundation. Used by permission. All rights reserved.

Scripture quotations marked NIV are taken from the HOLY BIBLE, NEW INTERNATIONAL VERSION®. Copyright © 1973, 1978, 1984 Biblica. Used by permission of Zondervan. All rights reserved.

Scripture quotations marked NLT are taken from the Holy Bible, New Living Translation, Copyright © 1996, 2004, 2007 by Tyndale House Foundation. Used by permission of Tyndale House Publishers, Inc., Carol Stream, Illinois 60188. All rights reserved.

Scripture quotations marked NKJV® are taken from the New King James Version®. Copyright © 1982 by Thomas Nelson, Inc. Used by permission. All rights reserved.

Scripture quotations marked NRSV are taken from the New Revised Standard Version Bible, Copyright © 1989, Division of Christian Education of the National Council of the Churches of Christ in the United States of America. Used by permission. All rights reserved.

Scripture quotations marked RSV are taken from the Revised Standard Version of the Bible, Copyright © 1952 [2nd edition, 1971] by the Division of Christian Education of the National Council of the Churches of Christ in the United States of America. Used by permission. All rights reserved.

Scripture quotations marked TLB are taken from The Living Bible®, 715800037417 Copyright © 1971, 1997 Tyndale House Foundation. Used by permission of Tyndale House Publishers, Inc., Carol Stream, Illinois 60188. All rights reserved.

Key Terms taken from the following:
www.thefreedictionary.com
www.merriam–webster.com
www.dictionary.reference.com

All rights reserved. No part of this publication may be reproduced, stored in a retrieval system or transmitted in any form or by any means—electronic, mechanical, photocopy, recording, or otherwise—without prior written permission of the copyright owners.

PAPERBACK: ISBN-13:978-1-68087-392-4 ISBN-10:1-68087-392-X
LARGE PRINT: ISBN-13:978-1-68087-389-4 ISBN-10:1-68087-389-X

The Prayer & Bible Band Topics is published quarterly by
The Church Of God In Christ Publishing House
806 E. Brooks Rd • Memphis, TN 38116

Table Of Contents

4		Presiding Bishop's Letter
5		Preface
6	Lesson 1	Stand for Righteousness
9	Lesson 2	God's Love and Care of Widows
12	Lesson 3	God Has a Place for Young People in Ministry
15	Lesson 4	Wisdom of Older Men and Women
18	Lesson 5	Seed-Time and Harvest-Time
21	Lesson 6	Treating Others Right
24	Lesson 7	Expect the Best From God
27	Lesson 8	God Heals Lepers
30	Lesson 9	Walking in Wisdom
33	Lesson 10	Chosen By God
36	Lesson 11	What is the Greatest Sin?
39	Lesson 12	Reasons for Going to Church
42	Lesson 13	The Kingdom of God for Believers

Contributing Writer

Written by Supervisor Lee E. Van Zandt

THE GUIDE FOR WEEKLY BIBLE BAND MEETINGS

For weekly Bible Band meetings, the President should plan each meeting one week in advance.

- Secure a leader for devotion who will make preparations.
- Meetings should never last longer than two hours; however, let the Spirit of God lead.
- Appoint a different spiritually-minded individual for the leader of the devotional service.

ORDER OF SERVICE

- Call to Order (by the President)
- Singing
- Prayer

SCRIPTURE DEVOTIONAL READING

- A Five Minute Talk (on the devotion by the leader)
- President's Remarks
- President Presents the Teacher
- Announcements and Remarks
- Singing
- Benediction

LETTER from the PRESIDING BISHOP

Greetings in the name of our Lord and Savior, Jesus Christ.

In this time of rapid change, it is vitally important for blood washed individuals to actively participate in our churches and communities to assure our voices are heard and God is glorified.

We must remain "steadfast, unmovable, always abounding in the work of the Lord, forasmuch as ye know that your labor is not in vain in the Lord".

With that being said, I want you to know, we have "Unfinished Business" in upholding our Christian duties and engaging in constructive dialogue to address societal challenges and the continued advancement of the Kingdom of God.

Our historical topic curriculum is filled with scriptures that will encourage and motivate you to keep pressing your way in the things of the Lord.

I encourage you to share the Word of God on every occasion and live so God can use you, anywhere and anytime.

Sincerely,

J. Drew Sheard
Presiding Bishop and Chief Apostle
Church Of God In Christ, Inc.

PREFACE

Time is filled with swift transitions; naught of Earth unmoved can stand. Build your hopes on things eternal, and hold to God's unchanging hand. As we move into 2025, we must recognize that things are changing. But, in the midst of changes, the believer remembers that he serves a God who is changeless. He is the same today, yesterday, and forever more, amen.

In this quarter, I believe God would have us explore practical things. His desire for His family is that each believer stay focused and hold to His unchanging hand. Stay out of the sin business. All unrighteousness is sin, and sin has penalties. Know what pitfalls we need to avoid. Hold fast to the Word of God, which will help you navigate a troublesome society. Our hope must be built on Christ and His righteousness.

Once again, I'm happy to tell you that I'm saved, sanctified, and filled with God's precious gift of the Holy Ghost. I thank our Presiding Bishop, J. Drew Sheard, and the General Board, along with our General Supervisor, Barbara McCoo Lewis, for the privilege of serving our Church as I once again write our Bible Band Topics.

Yours because of the blood of Jesus Christ that he shed for the remission of our sins.

Dr. Lee E. Van Zandt
Chaplain, Department of Women Executive Board
Elect Lady, COGIC World Mission Department
Supervisor, Maryland Eastern Shore Ecclesiastical Jurisdiction
Contributing Editor, *Prayer and Bible Band Topics*

Lesson 1 • First Week

Stand for Righteousness

Background Reading
Psalm 119:142; Proverbs 14:34; Matthew 5:6; Roman 1:17-20; 3:21-26; James 1:19-20

Devotional Reading
Romans 10:1-15

Central Verse

"He that followeth after righteousness and mercy findeth life, righteousness, and honor."
Proverbs 21:21, KJV

"Whosoever pursues righteousness, and unfailing love will find life, righteousness, and honor."
Proverbs 21:21, NLT

Key Terms

Lust—Usually intense or unbridled sexual desire; to have an intense desire or need.
Hunger—A strong desire; a desire or a need for food.
Imputed—To give the blame or credit to some person or cause.

Introduction

God made man in His image and likeness, which means that there is a part of him that only God can fill. Because of this fact, there is always a hunger in man for more than what he can acquire on his own or through worldly achievements. God wants man to recognize that he has a spiritual hunger that has nothing to do with natural food. He must recognize that his soul requires nourishment on a regular basis.

It does not matter how often a man prays or how many Bible passages he studies and memorizes. It does not matter how often he is in a church service. There will always be a hunger on the inside that cannot be satisfied until he realizes that the hunger is for righteousness. Jesus tells us he that hungers and thirsts after righteousness shall be filled (Matthew 5:6). That desire to get closer to God and learn His ways will constantly eat at a person when he has not been filled with righteousness.

What is righteousness? Is it an attribute that belongs to God? No man can be justified by his own works apart from God. Righteousness is a gift from God to humanity through His love. It is a God-given quality imputed to man when he believes and accepts the Gospel of Jesus Christ, the Son of God.

It is acting in accordance with the divine and moral law; it means free from guilt and sin.

Lesson 1 • First Week

Discussion

Many believers love God and the church, yet feel dissatisfied and empty emotionally, physically, and spiritually. They are low on joy, fulfillment, and peace. These are times when the enemy will deceive them and cause them to turn to sex, drugs, and alcohol. They know they are hungry and thirsty for something but can't seem to realize what it is. They don't realize that their spiritual appetite can become confused and do not know they need to change their spiritual diet. They need a change to bring wholeness, peace, and real nourishment.

John let believers know that all that is in the world is the "pride of life, the lust of the eye, and the lust of the flesh" (1 John 2:16). These three things are the driving forces in the body, and if a believer is not aware of his need for righteousness, he will allow that lust (or desire) to lead him to the negative things that will destroy him. Hunger has to do with the desires of the flesh and the spirit, so a believer must have the leading of the Holy Spirit within his spirit.

When a believer gets a spiritual diet change, he moves from tired, anxious, and overwhelmed to fulfilled, whole, and free. Righteousness exalts, but sin brings forth reproach. "When sin is fulfilled, it brings forth death" (James 1:15). Do not underestimate the persistent, clever, oppressive spirit of lust. It is important that the tactics of lust be exposed and the believer strategizes from a place of knowledge rather than from a place of fear to bring about defeat to that spirit of lust. Lust is savage and destructive, for it is of the devil. The believer needs to move into God with some "hungry prayers" that express their hunger for God and a depth of intimacy and closeness that only talking to God can bring.

Lust is a strong opposing force against righteousness. It is seen daily because the world is filled with advertisements that promote lust on every level. It is made to seem so common that it's difficult to avoid it. This world seems to try to trap every person by some type of sinful lust. The many sexual ads create lustful thoughts and the desire for sexual behaviors. The never-ending reality shows and movies about the lives of the rich and famous cause people to lust after fame and fortune. But there is hope for believers because they have Biblical truths that can help them overcome lust and receive true freedom.

The righteousness of God can and will help believers combat lust and allow them to live a lust-free lifestyle. They can walk in freedom from lust and stand for truth and righteousness. When a man loves righteousness, he will hate wickedness and iniquity and be blessed by the Lord.

When a believer stands for righteousness, pride cannot accompany him. Pride cannot lead the believer; it cannot promote him because it will impede his growth. To stand for righteousness, he must not just talk about the Word, read, or sit on the Word; he must live and deploy the Word daily, and pride will not allow him to do that.

Conclusion

The believer must remember that the wrath of man does not work within the righteousness of God. He must be careful what he allows to come out of his mouth and out of his spirit. A believer cannot get angry and just say anything because they will be accountable for their words and actions. "Be ye angry, and sin not: let not the sun go down upon your wrath" (Ephesians 4:26).

Lesson 1 • First Week

The believer must not be ignorant of God's righteousness, but they must submit themselves to God and His righteousness. The righteousness of God makes men aware that all men have sinned and have come short of the Glory of God. The righteousness of God allows men to know that Christ was the end of the Law.

Jesus was made sin for humanity because He knew no sin. He was born of a virgin, lived in flesh and was sinless, died and was buried, but on the third day got up out of the grave and is now back at the right hand of His Father. The just shall live by faith.

Questions

1. Why is it necessary for believers to stand for righteousness?
2. What ways will God help the believer stand for righteousness?
3. Why is righteousness of faith?

_____

_____

_____

_____

_____

_____

Essential Thought

If you stand for righteousness, righteousness will stand for you.

Lesson 2 • Second Week

God's Love and Care of Widows

Background Reading
Deuteronomy 10:18; 1 Kings 17; Psalm 68:5; 146:9; Isaiah 10:1-4; Jeremiah 49:11; James 1:27

Devotional Reading
1 Timothy 5:3-16

Central Verse

"Honor widows that are widows indeed."
1 Timothy 5:3, KJV

"Take care of any widows who has no one else to care for her."
1 Timothy 5:3, NLT

Key Terms

Honor—A showing of usually merited respect; to regard or treat (someone) with admiration and respect.
Practical Assistance—Help with everyday tasks, such as personal care and household chores that can help people maintain their independence and dignity.
Moral Obligation—A duty that a person feels they should do based on their own conscience rather than because of a law or contract.

Introduction

God has always shown love and made provision for the aged women. He especially cares for the women who served their husbands and their families and no longer have the protection of their husbands in the home. God's heart for widows is evident throughout the scriptures, and each believer has an obligation to learn from these scriptures and to put them into practice. A widow is a woman who lost her spouse by death and has not remarried. Caring for widows is not just a moral obligation but it is also a commandment from God. The Bible provides clear instructions on how widows should be treated and supported.

Discussion

There are several stories in the Old and New Testament concerning widows. One such story is found in 1 Kings 17. There was a widow living during this time and there was a drought in the land. Things had gotten bad, streams were drying up, food had gotten scarce, and like many other people, this widow was having a rough time. Her name was not given to the readers, she was described simply as a widow from Zarephath who had come to the end of her provision.

Lesson 2 • Second Week

She was picking up sticks to make a fire to cook her last meal for her and her son. The Prophet Elijah approached and asked her for a drink of water. As she prepared to get the water, he asked her to make him a cake. It was then that she informed him that all she had was a small amount of meal, and a little oil to make a cake that she was going to share with her son. Because she had no known support, she had thought that this cake would be her last and that she and her son would eat it and die.

She willingly shared what she had with the man of God, and because of her generosity and faith in God, God miraculously provided for her and her son during the rest of the drought and famine. There should not be any widows in our congregations who are suffering lack. The Saints of the Church should make sure that their needs are being met.

The Lord has commanded that the believers honor widows who are truly widows. Paul reminded the believers that they must care for these widows and ensure that their needs are being met and that they are protected by the Church. Jesus made provision for His mother when He was dying. He knew the responsibility of the children to see to the needs of their widowed mothers.

In Mark 12:41-44, Jesus pointed out a poor widow who came to the offering table and gave two small coins into the Temple treasury. It was a very small offering, but Jesus commended her for "giving all that she had." Compared to large donations, it may have seemed like she had not given much, but she was sincere and sacrificed to give what she had.

Many of our Pastors in our Churches use their livelihood to help grow their churches, help members, pay their dues, pay their utilities, and then die and leave their wives widowed with very little money to live on. I have seen widows struggle and become bitter toward God and the Church. It shouldn't be like this, but it is a fact of life. Sometimes, they marry someone else and are unhappy for the remainder of their days because little provision has been made for them.

The Lord let Israel know they had a responsibility to care for these widows who had no inheritance in the book of Deuteronomy. Taking care of the widows as well as the orphans is an important part of God's command, and it's important that our Church put something in place to meet this need. The Church must have people in place to give love and comfort to these women who have lost their husbands because many of them find it difficult to move forward with their lives.

Jesus took time with the widow of Nain whose son had died. While she was in the midst of her grieving, Jesus had compassion for her and raised her son from the dead. Can you imagine the grief she must have felt, already without her husband and now her son? She was on her way to the cemetery, thinking that this was the end. She felt hopeless, knowing that the grave was a final resting place, and the Son of God came to comfort and support her as she faced her tremendous challenges and gave her back her son.

We have another story of a widow named Naomi. After the death of her husband, she found herself a widow in a foreign land. Then, her sorrow was compounded because her two sons also died. Deep in grief, she decided to go home, taking her daughter-in-law, Ruth, not knowing what she was going to meet. She felt that she had left home full, but now she was returning empty, sad, and depressed, but she was met with such great kindness. The providence of God was there to meet her, for God had a cousin of her husband, Boaz, to be kind to her and her daughter-in-law Ruth, who was also a widow. God blessed her widowed daughter-in-law to marry her cousin Boaz and enriched her life with a grandson who gave her life.

Lesson 2 • Second Week

Conclusion

God wants believers to reach out to the widows in their own communities with love, compassion, and practical assistance. Give them a call, check on them, stop by and take a sweet gift, take time, and make them a meal. Sometimes, it's necessary to adopt some of these older widows who have no family and make them a part of a family. Help them to become involved with the families of the church. Give them opportunities to share their hobbies, skills, and wisdom with others. Many of them have much to share and to give, they just need someone to open the door for them.

Questions

1. Why does God have such love and concern for widows?
2. What are some of the things that believers can do to help widows?
3. What does" Honor the widows that are widows indeed" mean? (1 Timothy 5:3)

Essential Thought

Many times, widows have much to share; they just need
the opportunity to share.

Lesson 3 • Third Week

God Has a Place for Young People in Ministry

Background Reading
1 Samuel 3:1-20; Psalm 119:9; 148:12-13; Jeremiah 1:7; 1 Timothy 4:12

Devotional Reading
1 Samuel 17:31-37; 41-50

Central Verse

"And it shall come to pass afterward, that I will pour out my Spirit upon all flesh; and your sons and daughters shall prophesy, your old men shall dream dreams, your young men shall see visions."   **Joel 2:28, KJV**

"Then, after doing all those things, I will pour out my Spirit upon all people. Your Sons and daughters will prophesy. Your old men shall dream dreams, and your young men will see visions."   **Joel 2:28, NLT**

Key Terms

Siege—A persistent or serious military attack.
Meditate—To consider or think over carefully; to spend time in quiet thinking.
Mentoring—Being a wise and faithful adviser or teacher; being a trusted counselor or guide.

Introduction

The Word of the Lord tells young men that they are called upon because they are strong, and the Word of God abides in them, and they have overcome the wicked one. The energy and enthusiasm of youth can be a powerful force for good. They contribute fresh and new ideas because they live in an age of technology that many seniors do not have an opportunity to experience. The Bible recognizes the potential of young people to serve, live, and work for God. They have the ability, the skills, and the technology to make positive impacts on the church. It's important that they know they are needed and wanted in the ministry of the Church. The leaders of the Church must encourage and guide their youth so that they can be involved in the journey of faith and service.

The Apostle Paul admonished the young minister, Timothy, "Let no man despise his youth" (1 Timothy 4:12). Still, he told him to be an example of the believers in word, conversation, love, faith, clean living, and always remember the gifts that God had given him. He encouraged him to live a godly life, remembering that he was saved by the power of God. He encouraged him to study the Word of God and spend time meditating to be sure of his salvation. David informs the believers in Psalm 1 that if they

Lesson 3 • Third Week

want to be blessed, they must meditate upon God's Word day and night. Also, the Lord told Joshua that if he wanted good success, he must meditate upon God's Word (Joshua 1:8).

The world needs young men and young women who will be role models for other young people in the Church. God will help them by providing strength to those who call upon Him and allow Him to lead and guide them.

Discussion

The story of Samuel's call is an intriguing story about a young man that God called and used at a very young age. Samuel was brought to the Temple at a very young age and left there by his mother to serve the priest and learn the things of the Lord.

Samuel's mother had made a vow to God concerning him. Being the Godly woman she was, I'm sure she explained things to Samuel so that he could understand that she and her husband loved him, but his life was dedicated to God. Being a young child, I'm sure he had questions. But I believe that because God had destined him for this ministry, God had his mother and the Priest Eli to teach and train him concerning his place in ministry.

The Priest Eli spent time training and mentoring this young man in the ways of God and ministry. It is so important to train a child in the way that he should go. The leaders of the Church must take time and allow the youth to be active in every phase of the ministry of the church. The youth of today must know and feel the trust of their adult leaders. It is important that as they are brought and sent to the church, they understand the positiveness of what they, God, and the adults are doing. There are some areas in the ministry that might not be open to them, but transparency is very important to young people. As Eli began to become frail and his eyes began to become dim so that he could not see, the Lord began to speak to Samuel. Samuel and Eli had the kind of relationship that when God spoke to him, he could talk to Eli. He did not understand what God was saying, but the experience that Eli had with God, allowed him to be able to give this young boy the instruction that was needed.

Today's youth must become comfortable and respectful with their leaders so that when God speaks to them, they will know that their leaders will respect them and deal with them on a spiritual level. Because of the love and respect that Samuel had for Eli, he was able to receive the instructions that Eli gave to him. Because of this love and respect, Samuel became one of the most powerful Prophets of his time.

During the time of Kings, for Israel, God used eight young men as Kings over His people. Eight of the thirty-nine Kings that God put over Israel were young men and boys. God used Zedekiah, who was born in Jerusalem and began to reign at the age of twenty-one. Zedekiah was like some of today's youth who would not listen to his advisors. He created an alliance with Egypt. As a result of his actions and decisions, the King of the Neo-Babylonian Empire invaded Jerusalem and started a siege that lasted thirty months. All of this resulted in him seeing his sons killed, him being tortured and blinded and finally dying at a very young age.

God used Ahaz who was twenty and reigned for twenty years. Next was Solomon, who was also twenty; Jeconiah, who began at age seventeen; Uzziah, who was sixteen; Manasseh, who was twelve; Josiah, who began at eight; and one of the youngest to reign was Jehoash, who was only seven years old. Many of them did great things. Some made messes of their reign, but God gave them the opportunity to lead and be involved in the leadership of the nations. He wants the same things for today's youth, but it's according to the power that is working in them.

Conclusion

During the time when God decided to give His people Kings as they desired, it's noteworthy to note that He used older men, but He also used young men. Just as God found places of leadership for these young men, He wants to place youth in strategic places in ministry in His Church. But He needs young people who will be trustworthy, young men and women who will live as examples of holy living. Young men and women who will listen and receive instructions from the fathers and the mothers of the Church. He needs youth who will deny themselves, take up their cross, and follow Him.

Questions

1. Why does God need young men and young women in ministry today?
2. How can they be impactful in the ministry?
3. What are some of the things that helped Samuel to be so effective?
4. What are some of the things that can be done to involve the youth of today in ministry?

_____
_____
_____
_____
_____
_____
_____

Essential Thought

As God pours out his spirit, he uses sons and daughters
in the end-time ministry.

Lesson 4 • Fourth Week

Wisdom of Older Men and Women

Background Reading
Zechariah 8:1-8; Proverbs 17:6; 20:29; Joel 2:28; 1 Corinthians 2:1-16; 1 Timothy 5:1; Titus 2:1-8

Devotional Reading
2 Chronicles 10:6-15

Central Verse

"I said, Days should speak, and multitude of years should teach wisdom." Job 32:7, KJV

"I thought, those who are older should speak, for wisdom comes with age." Job 32:7, NLT

Key Terms

Rebel—To oppose or disobey one in authority or control; to renounce and resist by force the authority of one's government.

Wisdom—Ability to discern inner qualities and relationships; ability to see beneath the surface of things.

Introduction

Wisdom is very necessary in the lives of God's people. Wisdom is the quality of having experience, knowledge, and good judgment: it's the quality of being wise, according to the dictionary. Wisdom means that a person has the ability to interpret and understand knowledge. That person can discern inner qualities and relationships. Wisdom is a divine gift that God offers to those who ask him for it. The Word of the Lord tells the believer that if he has no wisdom, ask God for it, and he will give it to him (James 1:5). God will give the believer wisdom, insight, and direction for any season of his life. He is the one who directs the steps of Godly men and women. Wisdom doesn't come by wishing or hoping; it comes by asking God for it.

In today's world, we have all kinds of information at our fingertips, but sometimes, believers lack the wisdom to make good decisions and choices and miss out on the guidance that God wants to give them. The fear, respect, honor, and reverence of the Lord are the beginning and the starting point of wisdom. When a believer respects, submits and honors God, he will begin to reflect God's heart and character. Only the believer can allow wisdom to fill and lead his heart.

Lesson 4 • Fourth Week

The life of the Lord Jesus is full of depth, wisdom, authority, love, mercy, and life examples for anyone who really wants to know, follow, love, and obey God. Jesus's teaching transcends times and cultures. Youth and experiences don't go hand in hand; it takes time, experience, and God to bring wisdom into a believer's life. So, young people should seek the wisdom of older, godly men and women when making plans or decisions or when they have questions. Young people can't get wisdom from just anyone; they must be Godly men and women.

Discussion

God has several examples in His Word where younger people needed the wisdom of older men and women. In 2 Chronicles 10, the story of King Rehoboam was told. His father had been rough on the people and ruled them with a tight rein, but Jeroboam, one of the leaders of that time, went to him and asked him if he could lighten up some because his yoke was very heavy. He let them know that after three days, they could return, and he would have an answer for them.

King Rehoboam went and talked to the older men that had stood with his father, Solomon, and asked them for their wisdom and council concerning this request. They told him that he should be kind to the people, please them, and speak good words to them, and they would be his servants forever. But he did not accept the council of the old men. He took counsel with the young men who were brought up with him. Just as he had asked the older men, he asked the younger men, who told him to tell them that his fingers shall be thicker than his father's loins. He said that his father put a heavy yoke upon them and that he will put more to their yoke: he said that his father chastised them with whips but that he would chastise them with scorpions.

So, the next day, Rehoboam answered them roughly when he forsook the council of the old men but took the council of the young men, which caused the House of Israel to rebel against the House of David. If only he had listened to the wisdom of the older men, who had more experience and knew how to deal with life and its issues.

God has older, Godly men and women in His body here on earth for a purpose. It's to the younger believers' advantage to receive and accept the wisdom of the Church's fathers and mothers. Solomon said that the glory of young men was their strength, but the beauty of the old men was their grey head.

During Job's sickness, he was able to share with his visitors that wisdom comes through age. He let them know that with the ancient is wisdom and understanding. Old age is a time when men and women can remember and recall events, and they have time to dream dreams.

In the New Testament, the Apostle Paul instructed the church in the Book of Titus that the aged men should teach the younger men many life lessons, as well as the aged women should teach the younger women. He was very specific in what he needed them to teach. They needed to observe things in many areas of life. If they listened to the Seniors, their lives would be so much more enriched.

Conclusion

The wisdom of the Seniors will help younger believers have a more structured life, better personal relationships, better financial stability, and a much better well-rounded life. Psalm 92 tells the believers

Lesson 4 • Fourth Week

that the senior citizens who are Godly shall bring forth fruit in their old age, and they will yet be fat and flourishing.

The leaders of our Church of God in Christ were so wise, and they understood the value of the wisdom of the older men and women. They set up Bands, Auxiliaries, Units, and Councils where the older men and women could mentor the younger ones. They didn't call it mentoring, but that's what it was. They taught boys and girls in the Sunshine Band and Purity Class, the young women were taught in the Young Women's Christian Council, and the young ministers in The Bible Band and the Elder's Council. They taught everybody in the Young People's Willing Workers (YPWW) and Sunday School. They emphasized that as soon as you became a part of the Church, you automatically belonged to every agency of the Church.

Questions

1. What is one of the benefits of having Godly men and women in the church?
2. How can their wisdom help the overall well-being of the church?
3. Why did the nation of Israel rebel against the king?
4. What could he have done to change that?
5. What were some benefits of the older men and women's wisdom in the early church?

Essential Thought

Experience is a wonderful teacher, but why pay for something that you can get free?

Lesson 5 • Fifth Week

Seed-Time and Harvest-Time

Background Reading
Exodus 34:21; Ecclesiastes 3:2; Isaiah 55:10; Mark 4:2-20; 30-32; 2 Corinthians 9:10-11

Devotional Reading
Mark 4:26-29

Central Verse

"While the earth remaineth, seedtime and harvest, cold and heat, and summer and winter, day and night shall not cease."
Genesis 8:22, KJV

"As long as the earth remains, there will be planting and harvest, cold and heat, summer and winter, day and night."
Genesis 8:22, NLT

Key Terms

Sow—To plant seed for growth especially by scattering; to set something in motion.
Harvest—The season when crops are gathered; the gathering of a crop.

Introduction

The harvest is a time to celebrate and gather the joys of previous seasons, but some preparations must be made for this event. There are laws of the harvest that must be observed before a believer can reap his harvest. The believer must give bountifully and cheerfully to receive the abundance that God promised in His word.

Words are seeds that will produce if they are in the right setting. They produce one small seed at a time with God's help. Faith is a booster that, when applied right, will help seeds to flourish. For a person's life to be filled with love, joy, peace, patience, kindness, goodness, faithfulness, gentleness, and self-control, the person must have the "fruits of the Spirit" planted into his life, as recorded in Galatians 5:22-23.

Believer's lives are like spiritual gardens, waiting to become beautiful and flourishing. They need time and effort led by the Holy Spirit to work the soil by pruning, watering, and shining upon it. It takes time and effort to bring them to the place of fulfillment. The seed cannot be sown and brought to harvest until the soil has been prepared.

Lesson 5 • Fifth Week

Discussion

The sower of seed must make sure that his seed (Gospel) is being sowed into good ground. The sower sowed the same seed into four distinct types of soil and each one responded differently. It is important that the sower knows the kind of soil into which he is sowing. In the parable that Jesus shared, the sower sowed, and some of the seed fell by the wayside, and the fowls of the air came and ate it up. And some fell on stony ground, where there was not enough earth, and immediately it sprang up. Because there was not enough earth when the sun came out, it was too hot and scorched it, and because it had no roots it withered away. And some fell among thorns, and the thorns grew up, choked it, and yielded no fruit. Others fell on good ground; it wasn't too rocky, it had enough soil, and it was able to produce good fruit, which sprang up and increased and produced some thirty, some sixty, and some a hundred-fold blessing.

Jesus told His disciples that the sower sows the word and the enemy, Satan comes immediately and takes the word out of their hearts. Then there are some that were sown on stony ground, who, when they heard it, received it with gladness. But it didn't last because they had no roots in themselves to endure but for a little while. For the cares of this world, and the deceitfulness of riches, and the lusts of other things come in and choke the word, and it becomes unfruitful. But thank God there are some whose ground was good and who received the word and brought forth good fruit.

There is a process, led by the Holy Spirit, that will help the sower make the soil of the heart soft and receptive to God. Included in this process is the believer's communion with His Father God as he engages in continual conversation with his loving, heavenly Father.

This process includes a time for seeding, planting, and watering. Each cannot succeed without the other because they all work together to give good results. The presence, the will, and the love of God help the believers to allow their hearts to be tilled and become responsive. The Holy Spirit cultivates good soil so the world can produce and bear fruit. The Spirit of God breaks up the fallow ground, and the Word is sowed and produces fruit.

Grace is the seed that makes spiritual growth and maturity possible. Grace is simple, profound, and ever-growing, deeper and deeper than the believer can ever imagine. The believers were dead, but God rescued them so that they could have grace for the ages to come. With grace or the seed of righteousness, life, and discipleship are possible.

God gave the command to Adam to be fruitful and multiply. He has been consistent in His command and his persevering promise that through "Abraham's seed, all nations will be blessed." This is relevant to each believer today as he seeks to live in daily obedience to God's Great Commission. Our children are our seed, and David said that he had "never seen the righteous forsaken nor his seed begging for bread" (Psalm 37:25).

In Matthew 13:18-23, Jesus taught His disciples the power of words. The seed, which is sown, represents the Word of God. The ground receiving the seed symbolizes the condition of the hearts of mankind. The fruit that came forth is the manifestation of the Word. The words the believers speak impacts their lives and the lives of others. It is important that believers remember to speak positive things, for his words are seeds, and they will produce a harvest. Also, the power of life and death is in the tongue.

Lesson 5 • Fifth Week

Conclusion

God has made some promises to the believer, and one of them comes to reassure him that he will never have to worry. As long as the earth remains, there will always be seed-time and harvest time. He can count on the sun coming up, and certain things will be constant. God is so wise and caring for His children. He gave the command for Adam to work and dress the garden, but He also told him to take time and rest. The body cannot be healthy and produce all the things that God wants them to without proper eating and proper resting.

God has given man the right time to do everything he needs to do if he observes the correct time. He says there is a time and a season for every purpose under the sun. So, seedtime and harvest must be done at the appropriate time.

Questions

1. What do seed time and harvest mean?
2. What promises did God make concerning seed time and harvest?
3. What was the meaning of the parable of the sower that Jesus told?
4. What is some of the process of sowing and reaping?

_____
_____
_____
_____
_____
_____
_____

Essential Thought

God will always give seed to the sower and the sower must prepare for the harvest.

Lesson 6 • First Week

Treating Others Right

Background Reading
Zechariah 7:9; Joshua 2:12-14; Luke 6:36; 1 Thessalonians 5:12-18; Philemon 1:7-10; 2 Timothy 1:16-18

Devotional Reading
2 Samuel 9:1-13

Central Verse

"And be ye kind one to another, tenderhearted, forgiving one another, even as God for Christ's sake hath forgiven you."
Ephesians 4:32, KJV

"Instead, be kind to each other, tenderhearted, forgiving one another, just as God through Christ has forgiven you."
Ephesians 4:32, NLT

Key Terms

Tenderhearted—Easily moved to love, pity, or sorrow; compassionate.
Vitriol—Bitterly harsh or caustic language or criticism; something (as written or spoken words) thought to be as harsh and burning as acid.
Pervades—To spread through all parts of; permeate.

Introduction

Treating others right is a choice. A person chooses to be kind, thoughtful, and selfless because it reflects the heart of Jesus Christ. Having Jesus on the inside helps a believer to have greater self-compassion as he sees himself through the eyes of God. When a person learns to be kind and nice to himself, it's much easier for him to choose to be nice to others.

Now, remember there is a difference between being kind and being nice. It is easy to fake nice but hard to fake kindness because kindness is selfless. It is loving and genuine kindness is costly because it mimics Jesus. It lets others know that the old man of sin has been transformed. Striving to be kind is striving to be like Jesus. But when a believer can remember how kind God has been to him, he can respond by being kind to others.

Discussion

David had ascended the throne after the death of King Saul. Usually, when a new administration came into power on that day, they killed or got rid of all the families of the old regime. But because David was a "man after God's heart," he sought to do what was right, and that was to treat others right. There is an old proverb that says, "Do unto others as you would have them do unto you." This is a good proverb to pattern a person's life after.

After David got settled, he asked if anyone was left from the house of Saul so that he could show them kindness for his friend Jonathan's sake. This was not required of David, but because he wanted to remember the kindness Jonathan had shown him and because he wanted to treat people right, he pursued this question. When doing what is right is inside of a person, it's not hard to do what is right.

One of the servants from Saul's house was there, and he was able to tell David that there was a son of Jonathan who was lame on both his feet yet living. David enquired about his whereabouts and found that he was living in a place called Lodebar. David immediately sent for Mephibosheth, the son of Jonathan (Saul's son).

His first words to Mephibosheth were words of reassurance, letting him know that he was not there for any other reason but to be treated with kindness. This young man had experienced an unhappy tragedy in his life and, like so many people, needed some kindness shown to him. David brought this young man into his house, made provisions for him, and allowed him to sit and eat at his table.

The New Testament tells the story of a slave who had been mistreated, so he ran away from his master. He was blessed to meet the Apostle Paul and because of this encounter, he was introduced to Jesus and a better way of living. Sinner's lives should change when they meet a real Saint of God because we should be atmosphere changers. Believers do not have to participate in the atmosphere of vitriol that pervades the culture they are in. They should demonstrate the kindness of God in the way they treat others as well as what they say to others. They can make a difference by practicing intentional kindness in the midst of all the darkness in their culture.

Because of the kindness of this slave Onesimus, Paul wrote a letter to Philemon asking him to receive Onesimus as a brother. Paul acknowledged that at one time, Onesimus had been unprofitable to Philemon, but now he was a servant of Jesus Christ and was profitable to him and would be to his master. He asked Philemon to receive Onesimus as he would receive himself and if he had any debts to him, charge it to him (Paul). He asked Philemon to show Onesimus the same kindness he would show him, the Apostle Paul. Sometimes a kind word to someone in authority is all a person needs to get his life back in order to experience a better life. So be kind to one another, tenderhearted and forgiving one another.

Stop holding grudges against one another; let them go because if a person wants God's kindness and forgiveness, he must forgive others. Some people find it difficult to forgive others, especially if they feel the person wronged them without a reason. But whether there is a reason or not, believers must forgive those who trespass against them. Believers must make the decision to treat everyone right.

Conclusion

It's nice just to be nice, but it is even better to let someone know you are nice. Believers need to remember that they are the light of the world, and if anyone should be kind to others, it should be them. Our world is filled with darkness, evil, wicked, mean, and hateful people, and God wants His children to bring light, kindness, joy, peace, and happiness to those around them. A person can easily find a reason to ignore or be mean to others if they look for it. But they must let their light of love and kindness shine everywhere they go. It is with love and kindness that believers can draw the sinners. It doesn't cost much to be nice and treat others fairly.

Lesson 6 • First Week

Questions

1. How much does it cost a person to treat everyone right?
2. What are some of the benefits of treating others right?
3. Why does God demand that believers treat believers right?
4. Why must a believer be kind and forgive others?

Essential Thought

Believers must be righteous in every situation they find themselves in because they represent God at all times.

Lesson 7 • Second Week

Expect the Best from God

Background Reading
Psalm 140:8; Proverbs 10:28; 11:23;
Mark 11:22-24; 1 John 4:4

Devotional Reading
Romans 8:18-28

Central Verse

"Now unto Him that is able to do exceedingly abundantly above all that we can ask or think, according to the power that worketh in us."
Ephesians 3:20, KJV

"Now all glory to God, who is able, through His mighty power at work within us, to accomplish infinitely more than we might ask or think."
Ephesians 3:20, NLT

Key Terms

Earnest—Having or showing a serious attitude; not light or playful.
Expectation—The act or state of expecting; a looking forward to or waiting for something.
Great—Large in size; not small or little.

Introduction

The earth belongs to God. Mankind belongs to God. Everything in Heaven and Earth belongs to Him, and nothing is out of His reach. Jesus said when you pray, tell the Father to let His kingdom come here on Earth just as it is in Heaven. So, everything that He has in Heaven can be released for the believer on Earth. Whatever the believer binds in Heaven is bound on Earth, and whatever he releases on Earth is released in Heaven. Sometimes, believers receive nothing from God because their expectations are so low. The believer must remember that his God has everything and everything belongs to Him, and it is the Father's good pleasure to give His children the kingdom.

Jesus said ask, and it shall be given, but the believer must believe that when he asks, he will receive what he asked for. Just as the believers' children believe that when he asks his mother and Father for something, he is going to receive it, the believer should know that his Heavenly Father is going to give it to him.

Discussion

To expect means to think or believe something will happen or someone will arrive, according to the Cambridge Dictionary. It also means to think that someone should behave in a particular way or do a particular thing. To expect someone to do something or expect something from someone is part of the word to expect.

Lesson 7 • Second Week

To ask and receive from God, the believer must be positive in his thinking and use his faith in his expectation and use his faith to receive it. The Word of the Lord tells the believer it will happen, but it is according to the power that works in him. The Message Bible says, "God can do anything, you know—far more than you could ever imagine guess or request in your wildest dreams! He does it not by pushing us around but by working within us, His Spirit deeply and gently within us." Ephesians 3:20-21.

God had expectations of mankind, but they let Him down, so He put in place a power that could provide great expectations from mankind to Him. God so loved the world (mankind) that He gave His Son Jesus Christ to the world to die for their sins. God could not allow man to be in right fellowship with Him as long as sin separated them from God, so Jesus died to move the separation.

Romans 8:18 lets believers know that the sufferings of this present time are not even worthy of being compared with the glory which shall be revealed in each believer. For the earnest expectation, for all creation is waiting eagerly for that future day when God will reveal who His children really are. Against its will, all creation was subjected to God's curse. But with great anticipation, the believers look forward to joining Jesus in glorious freedom from death, decay, and the grave. They expect to become just like Jesus, with a glorified body, able to spend eternity with Him. The Lord knew that humanity was lost and desperate, without help or hope, and in need of salvation. But thank God for Jesus, who laid the foundation and opened up the way. As believers remain faithful to Jesus, they can enjoy an abundant life and maintain a greater hope in Christ Jesus.

When the believer feels that things around him are confusing, when it seems like difficulties are increasing, he's feeling weak and powerless. That is when he remembers that's not the end of his story. He has hope; he has great expectations; he knows that God, through Jesus, will give him the strength that will help him to withstand every storm that life can throw out at him. He knows that God has given him the very best that He has. Jesus is the best thing that could ever be in anybody's life.

God has given the believer the authority and the power to tread and to trample over the enemy in every area of his life. He is not defenseless against the wiles of the enemy. God has equipped him with the authority and power to defeat and overcome the snares and traps of the enemy in every area of his life. The believer has a right to expect the best from God, for God said in Isaiah 1:19," that if he were willing and obedient, he could eat the good of the land." In other words, he can have the best that God has to offer.

The enemy tries to make the believers feel they have no control over their circumstances. Satan wants them to be discouraged and feel depressed and helpless. God wants a believer to be inspired by His Word and His promises, expect and move on those promises, and watch every promise come to pass.

Conclusion

The believer has not lived his life trying to live Holy and living the best he can for God and does not have great expectations. He has denied himself the pleasures of this world because he expects to spend eternity enjoying the very best that God has to offer. He expects to live in a mansion in Glory, walking on streets of gold, looking at the pearly gates and walls of sapphire. He expects to see the foundation stones of jasper, sapphire, agate, emerald, onyx, carnelian, chrysolite, beryl, topaz, chrysoprase, jacinth, and amethyst. And above all he is looking forward to spending eternity praising and worshipping God with Jesus, the Angels, the disciples, and the saints from all the ages.

Lesson 7 • Second Week

Questions

1. Why can a believer expect great things from God?
2. What gives the believer confidence that God will give great things if he asks for it?
3. What does the believer classify as great things?
4. What is the earnest expectation of the believer?

Essential Thought

Don't just plan to go to Heaven, but expect to go there because it is the best that God has to offer.

Lesson 8 • Third Week

God Heals Lepers

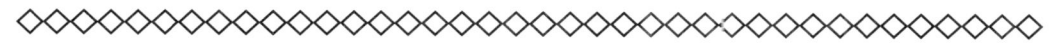

Background Reading
Leviticus 13;1-13; 2 Kings 5:1-14; Matthew 10:8; Mark 1:40-45;

Devotional Reading
Luke 17:11-19

Central Verse

"And many Lepers were in Israel in the time of Eliseus the prophet; and none of them was cleansed, saving Naaman the Syrian."
Luke 4:27, KJV

"And many in Israel had leprosy in the time of the prophet Elisha, but the only one healed was Naaman, a Syrian."
Luke 4:27, NLT

Key Terms

Unclean—Morally or spiritually impure; prohibited by religious law for use or contact.

Leprosy—A chronic infectious disease caused by a mycobacterium (Mycobacterium leprae) affecting especially the skin and peripheral nerves and characterized by the formation of nodules or macules that enlarge and spread accompanied by loss of sensation with eventual paralysis, wasting of muscle, and production of deformities.

Infirmity—The quality or state of being infirm or weak or frail in body (as from age or disease).

Introduction

Jesus came to seek and to save those who are lost; He came to set the captives free, and He came to heal those who are sick and afflicted. "Beloved, I wish above all things that thou mayest prosper and be in health, even as thy soul prospereth" (3 John 2). It is part of the reason He left His home in Glory to come and redeem mankind from the curse of the broken law.

In the early days, before we had modern medicine, many sick people died of different illnesses and diseases that we now have cures for. Leprosy was a bad disease during those days, and there was no known cure for it. Leprosy caused men and women to be separated from their families because they were classified as being unclean. But Jesus is the remedy for all kinds of diseases. Leviticus 13:9 says, "When the plague of leprosy is in a man, then he shall be brought unto the priest; and the priest shall see him: and, behold if the rising be white in the skin, and it have turned the hair white, and there be quick raw flesh in the rising; it is an old leprosy in the skin of his flesh, and the priest shall pronounce him unclean, and shall not shut him up: for he is unclean."

Discussion

Matthew 4:23 tells the believers that "Jesus went about all Galilee, teaching in their synagogues, and preaching the gospel of the kingdom, and healing all manner of sickness and all manner of disease among the people." He is the God of all flesh and there is nothing too hard for Him to do. Sometimes the Lord allows His children to get into situations that seem to be impossible to get out of. He allows sickness and diseases to come upon some of His people and they find out that the doctor has no known cure for them. That is the time they must know that King Jesus is a healer, and He is a doctor who has never lost a case. The late Bishop Gilbert E. Patterson used to say, "If you can have it; Jesus can heal it."

Jesus came preaching about the kingdom of Heaven and He let the people of that day know that He could forgive their sins and heal their bodies. He provided healing for His people just as much as forgiveness through His finished work on the cross. God has not made it difficult to receive a simple faith that focuses on seeing Jesus and what He has already done for the believers. He positions the believers for the power of God that is enough to heal every kind of sickness and every kind of disease, including those for which there is no known cure. There were a lot of sick and impotent people who had lost all hope of ever being whole again. But when they heard and saw the miracles that Jesus was doing, they began to follow Him seeking to be healed. The blind, the cripple, the deaf, the dumb, and those who had leprosy came looking for Jesus so that they could be healed. Seeing the multitude of people getting healed gave hope to those who had lost hope. The people began to understand that God was a God who was no respecter of persons, for what He had done for others, He was willing to do for them. So, men and women who had all kinds of sickness and diseases began to come to Jesus and receive their healing. Jesus' fame began to spread all over the known regions and the people came looking for Him. Among those who came looking for Him in Luke 17:12-19 were ten men who were lepers, which stood afar away from the people. They knew that being unclean, they could not come close to the people, so they cried with loud voices, asking Jesus to have mercy on them. When Jesus saw them, He said unto them, "Go shew yourselves to the priests."

As they obeyed Jesus and went, they recognized that they were cleansed. One of them, when he saw that he was healed, turned back and, with a loud voice, glorified God. He fell on his face at His feet, giving thanks: even though he was a Samaritan. Jesus answered and said unto him, "Were there not ten cleansed? But where are the nine? There are not found that returned to give glory to God, save this stranger." Then Jesus said unto him, Arise, go thy way: thy faith hath made thee whole.

Jesus told His disciples that as they went preaching the kingdom of heaven was at hand. They were to heal the sick, cleanse the lepers, raise the dead, and cast out devils: Freely you have received, freely give.

Conclusion

The book of Luke reminded the people that there were many lepers in Israel during the time of Elijah, the prophet, but none of them got healed except Naaman the Syrian. It was common to see people who had leprosy in that day, but they were not healed like they were after Jesus came. God can heal any disease that a beliver has, but they must have faith in Jesus Christ.

John the Baptist, the forerunner of Jesus, sent two of his disciples to Jesus and asked Him if He was the Messiah or did they need to look for another. At the time they arrived where Jesus was, Jesus had

Lesson 8 • Third Week

cured many people of their infirmities and plagues, and of evil spirits; the blind had received their sight. So, Jesus told them to go back and tell John the things they had seen and heard. He told them to tell John that the blind see, the lame walk, the lepers are cleansed, the deaf hear, the dead are raised, and to the poor, the gospel is preached.

Jesus has power over all disease. Out of the multitudes that followed Jesus, a leper came and worshipped Him, saying Lord, if thou wilt, "Thou canst make me clean." And immediately his leprosy was cleansed. Jesus said to him, "Don't tell anybody, but go your way and show yourself to the priest and offer the gift that Moses commanded, for a testimony unto them." (Matthew 8:2-4).

Questions

1. What was so different about leprosy from other diseases?
2. Why did the person who had leprosy have to separate themselves from their family and society?
3. What was one of the purposes of Jesus coming to the earth?
4. Who was the man in the Old Testament that God healed from leprosy?
5. After the leper was healed, why did Jesus tell him to go show himself to the Priest?

_____
_____
_____
_____
_____
_____
_____

Essential Thought
We serve a God who can heal anybody from anything.

Lesson 9 • Fourth Week

Walking in Wisdom

Background Reading
Job 12:13; Proverbs 1:7; 3:13; 13:10; 28:26; Ecclesiastes 8:1; 1 Corinthians 2:2-9; 3:19; 12:8

Devotional Reading
2 John 1:5-10

Central Verse

"Walk in wisdom toward them that are without, redeeming the time."
Colossians 4:5, KJV

"Live wisely among those who are not believers and make the most of every opportunity."
Colossians 4:5, NLT

Key Terms

Unique—Being the only one of its kind; being without a like or equal.
Susceptible—Capable of submitting to an action, process, or operation; easily affected.
Burnout—Exhaustion of physical or emotional strength or motivation, usually as a result of prolonged stress or frustration.
Precepts—A command or principle intended especially as a general rule of action.

Introduction

Wisdom is the quality of having experience, knowledge, and good judgment, the quality of being wise. It is the use of one's knowledge and experience to make good judgments. It is the interpreting and understanding of knowledge that leads to greater insight and common sense.

The Word of the Lord says "Wisdom is the principle thing: therefore get wisdom: And with all thy getting get understanding" (Proverbs 4:7). So, to walk in wisdom, the believer must make sure that he includes God and His infinite wisdom in his life, whether he is a leader or a follower. Without wisdom, every believer (leader or follower) is susceptible to isolation, discouragement, insecurity, and burnout. But that does not have to happen; for the Word of the Lord has a plan for pastors, ministers, evangelists, missionaries, and church leaders on every level who want to walk in wisdom and reflect Christ's character in their leadership. Every leader can receive God's wisdom for the unique leadership challenges they must face. As a leader, the believer must be able to provide wise counsel to the emerging leaders around him who crave wisdom. When he becomes wise while leading others, he can expand his influence and change lives by learning how to give wise counsel. God gives by His Spirit the Word of Wisdom to the believer so that the manifestation of the Spirit can give profit to that believer to help the body. The believer does not stand alone. He is a part of the Body of Christ.

Lesson 9 • Fourth Week

Discussion

God's wisdom is available to the believer. The word of the Lord tells the believer that if he has no wisdom or lacks wisdom, he should ask God for it. To make himself available to gain wisdom, go to the book of wisdom, the Book of Proverbs in the Bible. The need for wisdom is the one common denominator that every individual has. Wisdom is needed to make the big decisions and the day-to-day decisions in life.

The believer always has wisdom available to him. God's word is the greatest source of wisdom that a man can find anywhere he searches. The word of the Lord tells the believer that "the wisdom of this world is foolishness with God" (1 Corinthians 3:19). Having wisdom should be every believer's goal; for it is not just talking about intelligence or having above-average knowledge, but it is God's mindset that helps the believer consider and decide his path so that it can be aligned with God's will. Receiving wisdom will help the believer to grow in grace and in the knowledge of his Lord and Savior, Jesus Christ. But the believer cannot just go to any book and gain wisdom; he must be led by the Spirit of God. There are many educated people in the world around the churches, but all of them are not Spirit-filled and have no real understanding of the Word and the will of God. They will have a believer so confused that they will not be able to be victorious in anything they do.

The early Church had church mothers who would tell the Saints they couldn't eat at everybody's table and be whole. They stressed that you had to be careful about going to unauthorized Bible studies because, again, the wisdom of this world is foolishness with God. "There is a way that seemeth right unto man, but the end thereof are the ways of death" (Proverbs 14:12). So, to walk in wisdom, the believer must take heed that he doesn't get caught up with man's philosophies and strange doctrines that will cause him to be led astray. It is important that believers know what they believe, learn, and know their Statement of Faith.

James told the believers that "the wisdom that is from above is first pure, then peaceable, gentle, and easy to be intreated, full of mercy and good flesh" (1 John 2:16). He said that if a man has "bitter envying and strife in their heart, glory not and lie not against the truth. This wisdom did not come from up above, but it is earthly, sensual, and devilish. Where there is envying and strife, there is confusion, and every evil work" (James 3:14-16). And where there is evil work, know that the devil promotes it. Because the devil comes to steal, kill, and destroy.

Jesus Christ will help the believer walk in wisdom when he sees the importance of prioritizing wisdom and learns to experience wisdom in every situation daily. This causes the believer to walk in divine wisdom and good success as he pursues God's wisdom and becomes fulfilled in Jesus.

"The fear of the Lord is the beginning of wisdom" (Proverbs 9:10). It is vital to the well-being of the believer to build upon the principles and the precepts of God's Word as he walks in wisdom. The reverent and worshipful fear of the Lord is the chief and choice part of wisdom. So, the heart fears that the believer has and the honor that he has for God come together in a united front as he walks in wisdom.

Conclusion

As the believers read the book of Proverbs, they should become wisdom-challenged to unlock the secrets to a sustained approach of acquiring wisdom that profoundly changes them, as well as others.

Lesson 9 • Fourth Week

In his pursuit of walking in wisdom, the believer should put together a plan that is a simple, effective strategy for pursuing wisdom. Partnering in the pursuit and passing it along for impact. This should help develop a deep understanding and a deep hunger for the life-changing power of wisdom.

Proverbs is the greatest book of wisdom that a person can find anywhere. Most of it was written by the wisest man recorded to have ever lived. God gave His servant King Solomon this wisdom to pass on to the generations after him. The book of Proverbs embodies wisdom that will make the believer's walk of wisdom more effective and productive in every place he walks. "The blessing of the Lord, it maketh rich, and He addeth no sorrow with it" (Proverbs 10:22).

Questions

1. How can a believer walk in wisdom?
2. What are some of the influences that can affect the believer's walk?
3. Why is the wisdom of the world foolishness to God?

_____
_____
_____
_____
_____
_____
_____

Essential Thought

Don't embrace foolishness because if you do, you will walk in foolishness instead of wisdom.

Lesson 10 • First Week

Chosen by God

Background Reading
2 Chronicles 28:6; 29:10-15; Psalm 33:12; Isaiah 48:10; Matthew 20:16; Ephesians 1:3-4; 1 Peter 2:9-10

Devotional Reading
John 15:17-27

Central Verse

"Ye have not chosen me, but I have chosen you, and ordained you, that ye should go and bring forth fruit, and that your fruit should remain: that whatsoever ye shall ask of the Father in my name, He may give it you."
John 15:16, KJV

"You didn't choose me. I chose you. I appointed you to go and produce lasting fruit, so that the Father will give you whatever you ask for, using my name."
John 15:16, NLT

Key Terms

Forbearing—The act of holding back or keeping from; to be patient when annoyed.
Longsuffering—Patiently enduring lasting offense or hardship.
Flaring—To become very angry.

Introduction

What a blessing to be chosen for an inheritance by God. Sometimes, believers fail to recognize how blessed they really are. The Word of the Lord tells believers that they are a chosen generation, and they are chosen for a purpose. They are chosen first to show forth the praises of God. God has instructed everything that hath breath to praise Him, but He goes farther than that with the believers. He lets them know that their purpose is to show the praises of Him, who called them out of darkness into His marvelous light. When they were nobodies who had no mercy shown to them, He made them acceptable and made them His people by His mercy.

Many are called, but only a few are chosen. To be chosen by Christ means to be part of the eternal will and plan of God, to be positioned to impart God's will to humanity.

Discussion

With all the global and world problems it is important for believers to know that they are more than just ordinary people. They are extraordinary. God tells them that they are a chosen generation, not just another generation, because generations come and they go. They are not just chosen, but chosen by God. God wants each of them to understand their calling and use it as a blessing for the body of Christ. They should help His people in this confusing time to know the will of God for themselves as well as for others. They need to know why God has chosen this time for them to be here on earth. The believers chosen by God enter a priestly order, which puts the believer in a place where he must know that this high calling of priestly work positions him to be holy. They should be one of the instruments that God has chosen to do His work and to speak out for Him in this troubled society. He chooses believers who can tell others how God has made a difference in their lives. They should let others know how He has lifted them up far above the expectations of their families and the people who knew them. He has brought them from rejection to acceptance.

The Lord chooses people for His treasured possession. Out of all the people on the face of this earth, God has made choice of you: "For many are called, but few are chosen" (Matthew 22:14). The chosen ones are chosen even while they are in the womb of their mother. God told Jeremiah that He knew him before he was formed in his mother's womb, and before he came into this world, He had consecrated him and appointed him to be a prophet to the nation. That is one of the reasons the Lord lets the believer know that he didn't choose God, but God made choice of him.

Paul told the believer that he was blessed in Christ and every spiritual blessing by God the Father of Jesus Christ because, before the foundation of the world, God had a plan for his life. God has chosen for the believer to be in Him, holy and blameless before Him in love. Because God so loved the world, the believer so loves God.

God made choice of certain people because He knew that they would perform the job of being His witnesses. They would know and believe Him and understand who He is and know that He's the only God and there will never be another God who can measure up to Him (Isaiah 43:10). He knew that there would be certain believers whom He would call through His Son Jesus's gospel and that they would obtain the glory of His Son, Jesus Christ.

These believers will not have to tell others that God chose them; others will see and know by their lives that God has loved and chosen them (Psalm 82:6). For Paul said that God had opened His heart and accepted him into the beloved.

When a believer is chosen by God, he seeks to be like God. He seeks the holiness of God by having a compassionate heart and by showing kindness to all. Putting forth a spirit of humility, showing meekness, which is strength under control, filled with the works of patience. Able to take things without flaring up, able to forbear one another, loving enough to forgive. Seeking and having peace in every aspect of his life and always filled with thanksgiving, he must have thanksgiving every day, twenty-four hours a day.

Conclusion

To be chosen by God puts a person in a different category than just being a regular churchgoer. He must remember that he is not his own and can't just say anything. He is not his own, so he can't just go anyplace. He cannot connect with just anyone. He must ask God and allow God to lead him. He must remember that his steps are ordered by the Lord. Since he is chosen, he must acknowledge God and ask and receive His leading in everything.

Lesson 10 • First Week

They that are chosen are a part of the remnant chosen by God's grace, whom He has preserved for Himself, who will not bow to the things of this world, who will be an example of God's holiness and heirs of His riches and will be empowered through His grace.

QUESTIONS

1. How does a person know that he is chosen?
2. What is the difference between called and chosen?
3. What are some of the expectations that God has for those who are chosen?

_____
_____
_____
_____
_____
_____
_____

Essential Thought

To be chosen by God moves the believer
from ordinary to extraordinary.

Lesson 11 • Second Week

What Is the Greatest Sin

Background Reading
Psalm 92:15; John 7:18; Romans 1:17-18; 29; 9:14; 6:13; 1 Corinthians 15:56; 1 John 1:7-9; 5:16-20

Devotional Reading
Romans 7:7-25

Central Verse

"Therefore to him that knoweth to do good, and doeth it not, to him it is a sin."
James 4:17, KJV.

"Remember, it is sin to know what you ought to do and then not do it." James 4:17, NLT.

Key Terms

Atoned—To apologize.
Subsequent—Following in time, order, or place.

Introduction

Sin is a key concept in the Bible. All unrighteousness is sin. Sin is a rebellion against God in words, deeds, or desires. It destroys the relationship between God and humans and has disastrous consequences for people's relationship with one another and their natural environment. But know that God has a solution for the problem of human sin. Sin is a separator from God and all sin needs to be atoned. But some sins merit greater punishment than others. Jesus told Pilate, "He who delivered me over to you has the greater sin" (John 19:11).

Though Pilate would have to pay for the sentence that he allowed Jesus to receive, it was actually Caiaphas, the Jewish high priest, who coordinated the arrest and subsequent trial of Jesus (John 18:24, 28). It was Caiaphas, in conjunction with other religious authorities, who delivered Jesus into Pilate's custody.

Discussion

In the eternal sense, there is no greater sin, for all sin is sin because all sin separates mankind from his creator God. All sins are mortal sins in that even one sin makes the offender worthy of spiritual death and eternal separation from God. James 2:10 tells the believer that if he offends at one point of the law, he is guilty of all the law. Whosoever committeth sin transgressed also the law: for sin is the transgression of the law. We do not find in the scripture that there is the "greatest sin," but C.S. Lewis mentions in his writing that pride is the ultimate rebellion against God, and all the other sins are byproducts of pride. The Word of the Lord tells the believer that all that is in the world is "the lust of the flesh, the lust of the eyes, and the pride of life" (1 John 2:16). It is a proven fact that these three are destructive to the human being; for these are not of God, but of the world.

Pride is so bad that God names it among the six deadly sins that He hates in Proverbs 6. Pride has terrible consequences in the lives of believers, and it should be dealt with by completely putting it out of their lives. Believers know that God hates sin and evil, but because He is a righteous God, He tolerates it in His world. He has made it possible for mankind to know and realize that the wage of sin is death. He made man with free will to make his own choices, to choose Him and live, to choose sin and suffer the consequences of their choice. He gives man a choice in Deuteronomy 30:19 where He tells mankind, "I have set before you life and death, blessing and cursing, therefore choose life, that both thou and thy seed may live."

The Word of the Lord speaks of "the unpardonable sin" in Mark 3:22-30 and Matthew 12:22-32, and it is known as the unforgivable sin or "blasphemy of the Holy Spirit." Jesus said, "Truly I tell you, people can be forgiven all sins and every slander utter" (Mark 3:28), but then He gives one exception: "Whosoever blasphemes against the Holy Spirit will never be forgiven; they are guilty of an eternal sin" (verse 29). This sin occurs when someone knows the power of the Holy Spirit and denies it (Matthew 12:24).

The Word also speaks of the sinfulness of sin. Sometimes, because a person gets so caught up in doing the things of the world, he gets out of control and finds himself in a place that he never thought he would ever get to. Sin becomes so sinful that it controls his mind, thoughts, actions, and feelings. The devil will take a man farther than he ever thought he could go in sin and keep him longer than he ever planned to stay.

The prodigal son never dreamed that he would work a job touching swine, something no respectable Jewish man would ever touch. But when he got caught up in the sin business it robbed him of everything that was decent in his life. So many people have allowed themselves to become hooked on habits that get out of control. Sin becomes sinful when mankind loses all sense of right and wrong, when they will believe a lie and be damned. That is when men will have sex with their own child, whether male or female. It becomes sinful when a father is against his son and a son against his father. It becomes sinful when a mother is against her daughter and a daughter is against her mother. When men lose their natural affection for a woman and desire to lie with a man. And when a woman loses her natural desire for a man and desires to lie with a woman.

Conclusion

"The transgression of the wicked saith within my heart, that there is no fear of God before his eyes" (Psalm 36:1). Romans 3:23 tells the believer that "all have sinned and come short of the glory of God." So, as believers go through life facing inconvenient situations, which are filled with pain, failure, humiliation, and powerlessness, not finding correct answers, they become objects of the devil's power if they don't realize that their help and hope must come from God. God will give them the power to resist the devil so that the devil will flee from them. God does not want people to be caught up in the sin business. He wants them to flee from sin and all unrighteousness.

Lesson 11 • Second Week

It is important that believers take sin seriously, and know that every challenge, every discouragement, should not cause them to forsake their commitment to God and slide back into the sin business. They must be committed to Jesus and follow Him; for He is a rewarder to those who trust and obey Him. To avoid sin, our lives must be those which obey God's word and shun the very appearance of evil. With Jesus on the inside, the believer can find joy in every circumstance that they encounter. When Christ is their Lord, He gives them the power to overthrow the enemy in every area of their lives. When Christ lives in the heart of the believer, sin must bow, it must flee. The bondages of the past must go.

Questions

1. What is the greatest sin?
2. Why did Jesus tell Pilate that he had committed the greater sin?
3. What is the unpardonable sin?
4. What makes sin sinful?

Essential Thought

Sin is a reproach to any and all people.

Lesson 12 • Third Week

Reasons for Going to Church

Background Reading
2 Chronicles 2:3-7; Acts 15:4-6;
1 Corinthians 11:17:20; 14:23; Philemon 1:2

Devotional Reading
Ezra 5:8-17;
Hebrews 10:23-25

Central Verse

"I was glad when they said unto me, let us go into the house of the Lord."
Psalm 122:1, KJV

"I was glad when they said to me, 'Let us go into the house of the Lord.'"
Psalm 122:1, NLT

Key Terms

Tabernacle—A house for public worship; a tent used as a place of worship by the Israelites during their wanderings in the wilderness with Moses.
Tent—A raised covering over something for decoration or protection.
Church—A building for public worship and especially Christian worship; an organized body of religious believers.
Temple—A building for religious practice.

Introduction

For many years, the children of Israel wandered in the wilderness and could not build a stable place of worship. They used a tent as their tabernacle and moved it from place to place. They had been told to enter the courts of God with praises and to come before God's presence with singing. They knew that the place of worship was special, for God said that He had hallowed it and put His name there. The believers are called to gather in God's house and worship Him, but they are also called to help build and support His house. Each believer should be able to feel the call to action and help build God's house. Believers have a love connection for God, which causes them to be very protective towards Him.

It is very necessary that every believer build a relationship with God by getting a deeper understanding of His abounding love and His desire for each one of them to grow into a close personal relationship with Him. It can be done in a believer's home, but going into the Church gives him a closer feeling of God's presence because God's Spirit dwells in His Temple or His Church.

Lesson 12 • Third Week

Going to the church building gives a person a sense of belonging to a family and allows people to develop wholesome relationships that enhance their lives. It allows for spiritual growth. And they are fed with spiritual food when the preacher preaches or the teacher teaches. It is a place where information and understanding are given. It is a place where the gifts and talents of believers receive a place of training and exercise. The Word of God instructs believers to never forsake the practice of going to Church.

Discussion

Making the sacrifice of going to the church is giving God first place, which is a lifetime commitment that every believer must be willing to do. Each believer should learn to make attending church a habit by letting God work in his life. As he commits to going to church, he must commit to letting God build him, his family, his career, and every aspect of his life. The more he visits God's place of residence, the more he gets to know God. Going to God's House allows God to become involved in his life.

I personally can remember that I had gone to the doctor because I was having some physical challenges. I had been diagnosed with cancer, stage four. The treatment did not help me, and I was in much pain. Sometimes, I would say to my husband, "If I can just get to church, where the saints are." I knew the saints would be praying, praising, and worshipping God, and I needed to be in that atmosphere. Because I knew that somebody would touch God, and God would touch me. I attended one of our conventions (UNAC) in New Orleans, Louisiana that July. As I sat in the service that Sunday evening, the Spirit of the Lord spoke to me and said, "If you praise Me, I will heal you." Very reluctantly, after hearing the Holy Spirit repeat it to me three times, I leaped to my feet and began to scream Jesus repeatedly. While I was screaming Jesus, I felt the lumps in my breast began to move. In a matter of seconds, I could not find the lumps. I ran out of the sanctuary into a restroom, asked someone to unzip my dress, and proceeded to look for the lumps. Well, the lumps were gone! My breasts had turned from black and hard back to brown and soft. That evening, I received my healing. But if I had not gone to church, I probably would not have been healed.

Israel had been told that if they couldn't get to the church building, turn toward it and pray that God would hear and help them.

Life often presents unforeseen pitfalls that can throw believers off course. But believers must have a place of refuge and a place of anchor. When John F. Kennedy was killed, the family was looking for his mother. They found Mrs. Rose Kennedy in church. Her heart was hurting; her world was turned upside down, and the only place that she knew that she could go and receive the comfort and strength that she needed was her church.

The church is a place of healing for the spirit, the soul, and the body. So, in the trials and seasons of difficulty, the believer must hold the course to God and trust the process that renews and gives strength to the weary. The time that the believers are living in is a time of perils; it's a time of anxiety, fear, and worry. But in the House of God, there is rest for the weary. It's a place where people can come and lay down their burdens, fix their eyes on the Lord Jesus, and hear an encouraging word that will bring life to the dead issues in their lives.

For so many years, God's people had no beautiful house to worship in because the enemy had come in and stole all the beautiful vessels out of the Temple and destroyed it. God always has someone concerned about His house. King David wanted to build it, but God would not allow it to be so. But He did allow David to gather the gold, silver, brass, different types of wood, and all the materials needed to build it. But David's Son, King Solomon, had the privilege of building that beautiful temple.

Conclusion

Go to church anyway; for every believer has a past, and every sinner has a future. If you are having sex before marriage, go to church anyway. If you are a drug addict trying to beat addiction, go to church anyway. If you went out to the club on Saturday night and got drunk and stayed out most of the night, get up and go to church anyway. If you're having identity problems, not knowing if you want to be a man or a woman, go to church anyway. If you have a habit that you can't break, go to church anyway. If you are living with someone and can't turn that man or woman loose, go to church anyway.

The church is a hospital for the broken, the lost, the empty, the oppressed, the confused, the desperate, the indebted, and the rejected. God can take hold of a person and make something beautiful of their life.

Questions

1. What is the purpose of the Church?
2. Why should a person go to church?
3. Why is the Church called a hospital?

Essential Thought
The Church is the place where God's spirit dwells.
Meet Him, and He will meet you.

Lesson 13 • Fourth Week

The Kingdom of God for the Believers

Background Reading
Luke 9:2; 10:7-12; 17:20-25; Matthew 6:9-10; Mark 1:14-15; Acts 8:12; Hebrews 12:28

Devotional Reading
Matthew 6:25-34

Central Verse

"For the kingdom of God is not meat nor drink, but righteousness, and peace, and joy in the Holy Ghost."
Romans 14:17, KJV

"For the kingdom of God is not a matter of what we eat or drink, but of living a life of goodness and peace and joy in the Holy Spirit."
Romans 14:17, NLT

Key Terms

Joy—A feeling of great pleasure or happiness that comes from success, good fortune, or a sense of well-being.
Advent—The coming of Christ as a deity, the Son of God.
Kingdom—The eternal kingship of God; the realm in which God's will is fulfilled.

Introduction

The Kingdom of God is said to be the everlasting realm where God is sovereign and where Jesus rules forever. The book of Romans tells the believer that the Kingdom of God is not meat nor drink; it is not carnal things, nor tangible things that a person can purchase at a store, but it is righteousness, peace, and joy. It is those things that can only come from the Holy Spirit. It may include gladness and happiness, which is found in joy, but it is joy unspeakable and full of the glory of God. It is a peace that surpasses all human understanding and flows out of the Holy Spirit. It is the Holy Spirit on the inside working on the outside of man, and it is found within the heart of a believer.

Scripture shows believers that God is the undeniable ruler, the supreme being of the universe: "The Lord has established His throne in heaven, and His kingdom rules over all" (Psalm 103:19).

Lesson 13 • Fourth Week

Discussion

The Kingdom of God is righteousness. It is the quality of being right in God's eyes based on God's laws and standards. Righteousness is a gift from God to believers through Jesus Christ. For God so loved the world that He gave His Son, Jesus, to all who would believe on Him and accept Him.

Christianity.com says that righteousness, by human standards, is defined as "the quality of being morally true or justifiable." Justification is made according to the conformity of behavior with the regulation (or constitution, in the context of a nation).

In its deeper spiritual meaning, righteousness is the quality of being right in the eyes of God, including character (nature), conscience (attitude), conduct (action), and command (word). Therefore, righteousness is based upon God's standard because God is the ultimate lawgiver (Isaiah 33:22).

Righteousness is a God-centered attribute that cannot be obtained by any human effort. God tells the believers that His ways are not their ways, and His thoughts are not their thoughts. There is too much difference between the two. Righteousness is a God thing, and it is not about mankind at all. Man cannot measure up to God's righteousness in any way, shape, or form. Man does not have to strive to be righteous. He must accept the will and the mind of God by faith. Works do not attain it because it is a gift from God. Jesus told the believer to pray to His Father in Heaven and ask Him to allow His Kingdom to come here on Earth as it is in Heaven.

What the Kingdom brings to a believer is much more than what he can receive here on Earth. On Earth, believers strive to have food to eat, shelter, and clothing, which are just temporal things that will fade away. But the Kingdom shall last forever, throughout eternity. Righteousness exalts, builds, and sustains, because it is everlasting.

Jesus advised the believers to seek the Kingdom of God before they seek anything else. Most believers are seeking more, and most have expectations for their lives to be happy, to succeed professionally and personally, to be healthy, to overcome limits, and to live a better life. Well, Jesus said if you seek the Kingdom of God — the righteousness, peace, and joy in the Holy Spirit — everything else that you need will be added to your life. God wants every believer to be happy, complete, and prosperous in every area of their life. God knows that apart from Him, the believer's life is incomplete.

The Kingdom of God is peace, tranquility, harmony, security, prosperity, or well-being. It is a desired status in relationships between God, mankind, and oneself. Peace is so important in the Kingdom of God that the believers were told to follow peace with all men and holiness, without which no one shall see the Lord. He told the believers to go after peace, pursue peace, and find peace, for where there is peace, the blessing of the Lord abides. Jesus is the Prince of Peace; He is what everyone seeking for the Kingdom of God needs and desires (Isaiah 9:6). This peace will keep the heart and mind of the believer secure. So, as the believer seeks the Kingdom of God, he must believe, receive, and embrace the advent of Jesus Christ. Let the peace of God rule in your heart (Colossians 3:15).

The Kingdom of God is joy, which is a choice; the believer must choose to be content and satisfied as he goes through trials and negative circumstances that normally would not be a time of joy and contentment. But with the Holy Spirit, the believer receives power to do what seems impossible. The Holy Spirit will give the believer a garment of praise for the spirit of heaviness. The Kingdom supplies joy in the midst of sorrow, creating hope when the believer sees no tomorrow. Because the Holy Spirit gives joy, it is not based on human actions, so human actions cannot shake joy out of believers' lives.

Conclusion

So, as believers, seek the kingdom of God and know that it can be found. If a believer believes in God as Scripture has said, he will find that the kingdom of God is within himself. The Holy Spirit will walk and talk with them. The Holy Spirit will make Himself known in every possible way, and the believer can say, "This joy that I have, the world didn't give it to me, and the world can't take it away. God is the originator of true joy."

So, he seeks not food and clothes, but a city, the place Jesus calls home—His Father's House, the place whose builder and maker is God. The place where he can spend eternity, the Kingdom of God, righteousness, peace, and joy in the Holy Ghost.

Questions

1. What is the Kingdom of God?
2. Who can have the Kingdom of God?
3. What makes up the Kingdom of God?
4. Why is righteousness a part of the Kingdom of God?
5. Why is joy a choice?

_____
_____
_____
_____
_____
_____

Essential Thought

It's alright to seek things that will comfort you, but make sure you have the Comforter first.

NOTES

The Presiding Bishop, Chairman of the Publishing Board, General Supervisor of the Department of Women, Contributing Writers, and the entire Prayer & Bible Band Topics Editorial Staff would like to thank you for your continued support.

Bishop J. Drew Sheard
Presiding Bishop

Bishop Uleses C. Henderson, Jr.
Chairman, Publishing Board

Mother Barbara McCoo Lewis
*General Supervisor,
Department of Women*

Supervisor Lee Etta Van Zandt
Contributing Writer

Supervisor Francis S. Curtis
Contributing Writer

Elder Joseph W. Gill
Contributing Writer

1-877-746-8578 | WWW.COGICPUBLISHINGHOUSE.NET

Church Of God In Christ Doctrine

THE BIBLE
We believe that the Bible is the Word of God and contains one harmonious and sufficiently complete system of doctrine. We believe in the full inspiration of the Word of God. We hold the Word of God to be the only authority in all matters and assert that no doctrine can be true or essential, if it does not find a place in this Word.

THE FATHER
We believe in God, the Father Almighty, the Author and Creator of all things. The Old Testament reveals God in diverse manners, by manifesting His nature, character, and dominions. The Gospels in the New Testament give us knowledge of God the "Father" or "My Father", showing the relationship of God to Jesus as Father, or representing Him as the Father in the Godhead, and Jesus Himself that Son (John 15:8, 14:20). Jesus also gives God the distinction of "Fatherhood" to all believers when He explains God in the light of "Your Father in Heaven" (Matthew 6:8).

THE SON
We believe that Jesus Christ is the Son of God, the Second person in the Godhead of the Trinity or Triune Godhead. We believe that Jesus was and is eternal in His person and nature as the Son of God who was with God in the beginning of creation (John 1:1). We believe that Jesus Christ was born of a virgin called Mary according to the Scripture (Matthew 1:18), thus giving rise to our fundamental belief in the Virgin Birth and to all of the miraculous events surrounding the phenomenon (Matthew 1:18–25). We believe that Jesus Christ became the "suffering servant" to man; this suffering servant came seeking to redeem man from sin and to reconcile him back to God, his Father (Romans 5:10). We believe that Jesus Christ is standing now as mediator between God and man (I Timothy 2:5)

THE HOLY GHOST
We believe the Holy Ghost or Holy Spirit is the third person of the Trinity, proceeds from the Father and the Son, is of the same substance, equal to power and glory, and is together with the Father and the Son, to be believed in, obeyed, and worshipped. The Holy Ghost is a gift bestowed upon the believer for the purpose of equipping and empowering the believer, making him a more effective witness for service in the world. He teaches and guides one into all truth (John 16:13; Acts 1:8, 8:39).

THE BAPTISM OF THE HOLY GHOST
We believe that the Baptism of the Holy Ghost is an experience subsequent to conversion and sanctification and that tongue–speaking is the consequence of the baptism in the Holy Ghost with the manifestations of the fruit of the spirit (Galatians 5:22–23; Acts 10:46, 19:1–6). We believe that we are not baptized with the Holy Ghost in order to be saved but that we are baptized with the Holy Ghost because we are saved. (Acts 19:1–6; John 3:5). When one receives a baptismal Holy Ghost experience, we believe one will speak with a tongue unknown to oneself according to the sovereign will of Christ. To be filled with the Spirit means to be Spirit controlled as expressed by Paul in Ephesians 5:18–19. Since the charismatic demonstrations were necessary to help the early church to be successful in implementing the command of Christ, we therefore, believe that a Holy Ghost experience is mandatory for all men today.

MAN
We believe that man was created Holy by God, composed of body, soul, and spirit. We believe that man, by nature, is sinful and unholy. Being born in sin, he needs to be born again, sanctified and cleansed from all sins by the Blood of Jesus. We believe that man is saved by confessing and forsaking his sins, and believing on the Lord Jesus Christ, and that having become a child of God, by being born again and adopted into the family of God, he may, and should, claim the inheritance of the sons of God, namely the baptism of the Holy Ghost.

SIN
Sin, the Bible teaches, began in the angelic world (Ezekiel 28:11–19; Isaiah 14:12–20), and is transmitted into the blood of the human race through disobedience and deception motivated by unbelief (I Timothy 2:14). Adam's sin, committed by eating of the forbidden fruit from the tree of knowledge of good and evil, carried with it permanent pollution or depraved human nature to all his descendants. This is called "original sin." Sin can now be defined as a volitional transgression against God and a lack of conformity to the will of God. We, therefore, conclude that man by nature, is sinful and that he has fallen from a glorious and righteous state from which he was created, and has become unrighteous and unholy. Man, therefore, must be restored to his state of holiness from which he has fallen by being born again (John 3:7).

SALVATION
Salvation deals with the application of the work of redemption to the sinner and with his restoration to divine favor and communion with God. This redemptive operation of the Holy Ghost upon sinners is brought about by repentance toward God and faith toward our Lord Jesus Christ which brings conversion, Faith, Justification Regeneration, Sanctification, and the Baptism of the Holy Ghost. Repentance is the work of God, which results in a change of mind in respect to man's relationship to God. (Matthew 3:1–2, 4:17; Acts 20:21). Faith is a certain conviction wrought in the heart by the Holy Spirit, as to the truth of the Gospel and a heart trust in the promises of God in Christ (Romans 1:17, 3:28; Matthew 9:22; Acts 26:18). Conversion is that act of God whereby He causes the regenerated sinner, in his conscious life, to turn to Him in repentance and faith (II Kings 5:15; II Chronicles 33:12–13; Luke 19:8–9; Acts 8:30). Regeneration is that act of God by which the principle of the new life is implanted in man, and the governing disposition of soul is made holy and the first holy exercise of this new disposition is secured. Sanctification is that gracious and continuous operation of the Holy Ghost, by which He delivers the justified sinner from the pollution of sin, renews his whole nature in the image of God and enables him to perform good works (Romans 6:4, 5:6; Colossians 2:12, 3:1).

ANGELS
The Bible uses the term "angel" (a heavenly body) clearly and primarily to denote messengers or ambassadors of God with such Scripture references as Revelations 4:5, which indicates their duty in heaven to praise God (Psalm 103:20), to do God's will (Matthew 18:10) and to behold His face. But since heaven must come down to earth, they also have a mission to earth. The Bible indicates that they accompanied God in the Creation, and also that they will accompany Christ in His return in Glory.

DEMONS
Demons denote unclean or evil spirits; they are sometimes called devils or demonic beings. They are evil spirits, belonging to the unseen or spiritual realm, embodied in human beings. The Old Testament refers to the prince of demons, sometimes called Satan (Adversary) or Devil, as having power and wisdom, taking the habitation of other forms such as the serpent (Genesis 3:1). The New Testament speaks of the Devil as Tempter (Matthew 4:3) and it goes on to tell the works of Satan, The Devil, and Demons as combating righteousness and good in any form, proving to be an adversary to the saints. Their chief power is exercised to destroy the mission of Jesus Christ. It can well be said that the Christian Church believes in Demons, Satan, and Devils. We believe in their power and purpose. We believe they can be subdued and conquered as in the commandment to the believer by Jesus. " In my name they shall cast out devils;" and the work of the Devil and to resist him and then he will flee (WITHDRAW) from you. (Mark 16:17).

THE CHURCH
The Church forms a spiritual unity of which Christ is the divine head. It is animated by one Spirit, the Spirit of Christ. It professes one faith, shares one hope, and serves one King. It is the citadel of the truth and God's agency for communicating to believers all spiritual blessings. The Church then is the object of our faith rather than of knowledge. The name of our Church, "CHURCH OF GOD IN CHRIST" is supported by I Thessalonians 2:14 and other passages in the Pauline Epistles. The word "CHURCH" or "EKKLESIA" was first applied to the Christian society by Jesus Christ in Matthew 16:18, the occasion being that of his benediction of Peter at Caesarea Philippi.

THE SECOND COMING OF CHRIST
We believe in the second coming of Christ; that He shall come from heaven to earth, personally, bodily, visibly (Acts 1:11; Titus 2:11–13; Matthew 16:27; 24:30; 25:30; Luke 21:27, John 1:14, 17, Titus 2:11) and that the Church, the bride, will be caught up to meet Him in the air (I Thessalonians 4:16–17). We admonish all who have this hope to purify themselves as He is pure.

DIVINE HEALING
The Church Of God In Christ believes in and practices Divine Healing. It is a commandment of Jesus to the Apostles (Mark 16:18). Jesus affirms His teachings on healing by explaining to His disciples, who were to be Apostles, that healing the afflicted is by faith (Luke 9:40–41). Therefore, we believe that healing by faith in God has scriptural support and ordained authority. St. James' writings in his epistle encourage Elders to pray for the sick, lay hands upon them and to anoint them with oil, and that prayers with faith shall heal the sick and the Lord shall raise them up. Healing is still practiced widely and frequently in the Church Of God In Christ, and testimonies of healing in our Church testify to this fact.

MIRACLES
The Church Of God In Christ believes that miracles occur to convince men that the Bible is God's Word. A miracle can be defined as an extraordinary visible act of Divine power, wrought by the efficient agency of the will of God, which has as its final cause the vindication of the righteousness of God's Word. We believe that the works of God, which were performed during the beginnings of Christianity, do and will occur even today where God is preached, Faith in Christ is exercised, The Holy Ghost is active, and the Gospel is promulgated in the truth (Acts 5:15, 6:8, 9:40; Luke 4:36, 5:5–6, 7:14–15; Mark 14:15).

THE ORDINANCES OF THE CHURCH
It is generally admitted that for an ordinance to be valid, it must have been instituted by Christ. When we speak of ordinances of the Church, we are speaking of those instituted by Christ, in which by sensible signs the grace of God in Christ, and the benefits of the covenant of grace are represented, sealed, and applied to believers, and these in turn give expression to their faith and allegiance to God. The Church Of God In Christ recognizes three ordinances as having been instituted by Christ Himself and therefore, binding upon the Church practice.

A. THE LORD'S SUPPER (HOLY COMMUNION)
The Lord's Supper symbolizes the Lord's death and suffering for the benefit and in the place of His people. It also symbolizes the believer's participation in the crucified Christ. It represents not only the death of Christ as the object of faith which unites the believers to Christ, but also the effect of this act as the giving of life, strength, and joy to the soul. The communicant by faith enters into a special spiritual union of his soul with the glorified Christ.

B. FEET WASHING
Feet Washing is practiced and recognized as an ordinance in our Church because Christ, by His example, showed that humility characterized greatness in the Kingdom of God, and that service, rendered to others gave evidence that humility, motivated by love, exists. These services are held subsequent to the Lord's Supper; however, its regularity is left to the discretion of the Pastor in charge.

C. WATER BAPTISM
We believe that Water Baptism is necessary as instructed by Christ in John 3:5, "UNLESS MAN BE BORN AGAIN OF WATER AND OF THE SPIRIT."

However, we do not believe that water baptism alone is a means of salvation, but is an outward demonstration that one has already had a conversion experience and has accepted Christ as his personal Savior. As Pentecostals, we practice immersion in preference to "SPRINKLING", because immersion corresponds more closely to the death, burial, and resurrection of our Lord (Colossians 2:12). It also symbolizes regeneration and purification more than any other mode. Therefore, we practice immersion as our mode of Baptism. We believe that we should use the Baptismal Formula given us by Christ for all "...IN THE NAME OF THE FATHER, AND OF THE SON, AND OF THE HOLY GHOST." (Matthew 28:19)

The Church Of God In Christ Statement Of Faith

We believe the Bible to be the inspired and only infallible written Word of God.
We believe that there is only One God, eternally existent in three persons: God the Father, God the Son, and God the Holy Spirit.
We believe in the blessed Hope, which is the rapture of the Church of God, which is in Christ, at His return.
We believe that the only means of being cleansed from sin is through repentance and faith in the precious Blood of Jesus Christ.
We believe that regeneration by the Holy Ghost is absolutely essential for personal salvation.
We believe that the redemptive work of Christ on the Cross provides healing for the human body in answer to believing prayer.
We believe that the Baptism of the Holy Spirit, according to Acts 2:4, is given to believers who ask for it.
We believe in the sanctifying power of the Holy Spirit, by whose indwelling the Christian is enabled to live a holy and separated life in this present world.